MW00332867

I dedicate this book to all children who are, without their choice, caught in the middle of parental conflicts ...

Acknowledgements

I would like to thank my loving husband, Leonardo, for his belief in me, for motivating me, and for supporting me while I wrote this book. Also, special thanks to my father, Robert, who was the first to read the story of Nina, for his unconditional support. And last but not least my sister Esther, and my friend Caroline for their suggestions to improve the book.

Introduction for parents: how to use this book

Divorce or separation is a stressful process and a time of change for all members of the family. Everything that once felt familiar and safe now feels unsafe and uncertain. For you as a parent, that means letting go of the dream to grow old together. It means moving, splitting all assets and liabilities, adjusting to a new financial situation, getting used to being single again, changes in your social life, and dealing with all the emotions that accompany all these changes.

Sometimes, as a parent, you need so much energy to cope with the changes you are going through, both emotional and material, that you may forget to explain to your children what is going to change for them and how this might make them feel. As a newly divorced parent, you may simply not be able to foresee what is going to change for your child (and yourself) yet. Sometimes parents have the misconception that the child will not understand if they try to explain what is going on. Truth is that children can understand more than you think if you talk to them in developmentally appropriate language.

I realize that it is not possible to personalize this book to all unique situations. That is not the purpose of the book. What this book can do is help you explain to the child what he or she might be going through. It can give you a frame of reference and tools to discuss the issues children are dealing with while you are going through a divorce. Ideally, the child reads the book with each parent so the topic can be discussed with both of you.

This book shows how Nina struggles with emotions of sadness, separation anxiety, anger, and guilt caused by the separation. It shows the ambivalence of Nina toward the parent she is visiting and the parent she has to leave behind. These are feelings that most children experience while going through a divorce, and most children in this situation will identify with Nina. It shows the advantages and the disadvantages of having two houses. Like almost every child in a divorce situation, Nina is loyal to both parents and has reconciliation fantasies about her parents.

Before you start reading this book with your child, make sure the atmosphere is right. Find a quiet moment and a comfortable spot to sit with your child. Most young children like to sit on their parent's lap or cuddle up next to them while parents are reading. Young children see themselves as the center of the universe, and they might make remarks about their own situation while reading the book ("I have two houses too" or "My daddy left to another house too"). This is to be expected.

Listen to what your child has to say and try to respond in an affirmative and reassuring way before continuing with the story. That way the child knows this is a topic he or she can safely discuss with you. Even though you have your own version of events, try not to bring up your own feelings toward the divorce or your ex. By simply listening to your child and accepting his or her feelings and thoughts, you send your child the message that what he or she has to say is valuable and worthy of being listened to. Doing this will not only have a positive effect on your child's self-esteem, but also build the trust between you and your child.

You can also use elements from the story to generalize these into your child's daily life by referring to the main character when one of the topics is appropriate. For example, if your child comes home from a visitation with the other parent and is upset, you can ask questions to help your child give words to his or her emotions. If asking "What happened?" doesn't get you any response, you can say, for example: "I know it is not easy to live in two houses. Remember Nina? She missed her mommy when she was with Daddy. Did you miss Mommy too? Nina felt sad to say good-bye to Daddy. Did you feel sad to say bye to Daddy as well?"

The book can also be used to give stepsiblings or friends of all ages insight into the world of their peers whose parents are going through a divorce.

All family situations and all children are unique; not all children and parents will have the same experience while reading this book. If you create a positive interaction with your child when reading this book, while giving words and understanding to emotions in a confusing time full of conflicting feelings, you are making it easier for your child to adjust to the new situation. ∎

Nina is four years old. She has a mommy and a daddy, but her mommy and her daddy don't live in the same house. Mommy has a house, and Daddy has another house. Nina lives with Mommy some days, and other days she lives with Daddy.

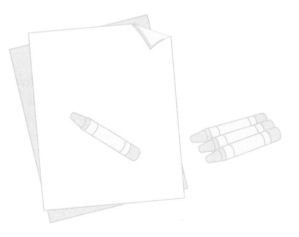

When Nina was two years old, Nina's mommy and daddy lived in the same house with Nina. They used to play with the blocks and read Nina her favorite books. Playing with Mommy and Daddy made her feel happy.

But Nina's mommy and daddy didn't get along. They used to say bad things to each other. Sometimes Nina heard them talking with angry voices, and this made her feel sad and also scared. Sometimes Nina would cry.

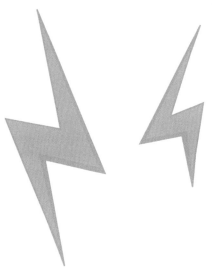

When Nina and her best friend, Katy, fight over a toy, Mommy always says, "Don't fight. Play nice." Then Nina and Katy make up and are friends again. Nina said, "Don't fight. Play nice," to Mommy and Daddy. With Mommy and Daddy that didn't help, though. They didn't make up. They still had angry faces.

Then Nina's daddy left to another house. Nina's mommy and daddy didn't want to live in the same house anymore. Before he left, Daddy said he still loved Nina, but he looked sad.

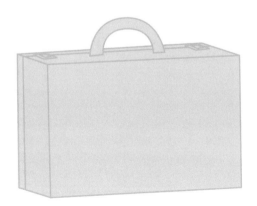

Nina is afraid her mommy will leave as well. This makes her feel scared. Mommy tells her that she doesn't have to worry about that. Mommy will always take care of Nina, and she should not be afraid to be alone. Mommy loves Nina very much.

When Nina is with Daddy, he tells her that he wants to see her as much as possible. They eat in front of the television in Daddy's house. With Mommy, she has to sit at the table and go to bed at eight. With Daddy, she can stay up real late.

Nina notices her mommy looks sad, and Nina notices her daddy looks sad. She doesn't understand. She feels angry and kicks her toys sometimes. She wants Mommy and Daddy to live together and be happy again!

Sometimes Nina comes back from Daddy tired and confused. All the changes make her want to act like a baby again. She wants to drink from a bottle, and all she wants to do is cuddle up on Mommy's lap. Sometimes she even wets her pants. Mommy understands that there are many changes for Nina.

When Nina is in her bed and it is time to say "night-night," she can't fall asleep. She wishes that Mommy and Daddy would live in the same house again. Sometimes she cries. When she gets a hug, she feels a little better.

Sometimes Nina thinks that it is her fault that Mommy and Daddy don't live in the same house anymore. She feels sad when she thinks about it. Daddy told Nina, "It is not your fault that Daddy lives in another house. Mommy and Daddy love you very much, but we don't like to live together anymore."

Now Nina has two houses! She has two beds, two bicycles, and two dollhouses. In Mommy's house Nina has lots of toys, and in Daddy's house she also has lots of toys. Nina feels that she is a lucky girl! She feels happy when she plays with her toys.

Nina likes to go to Daddy's house. He hugs her, plays with her, and buys her ice cream. Nina feels sad to leave her Mommy when she goes to Daddy's with her backpack. She doesn't like to see her mommy with a sad face.

Sometimes Nina cries, "I don't want to go to Daddy!" because she feels sad to leave Mommy. Mommy says she doesn't have to worry about her. Mommy will be fine.

When Nina is with Daddy, she misses Mommy. When Nina is with Mommy, she misses Daddy. Nina wants Mommy and Daddy to live in the same house again. Mommy and Daddy say, "that is not going to happen."

Sometimes Nina wants to play with her doll Sophie when she is in Mommy's house. Mommy tells her that Sophie is in Daddy's house and she has to wait until she goes to Daddy's again. Nina wants Sophie NOW and cries. It is not easy to have two houses!

Today is Nina's birthday. She is turning five years old. She gets to celebrate her birthday two times! She gets two cakes, one at Mommy's house and one at Daddy's house. Nina loves to eat cake.

It is gift-time at Mommy's house and gift-time at Daddy's house. Nina gets hugs from Mommy, and she gets hugs from Daddy. Nina plays with her new toys. They all smile and Nina feels happy.

The end

Advise for divorced parents

1. Unfortunately, a divorce is difficult for all children caught in the middle. Know that children are resilient and will be able to adjust with time. Remember that ongoing conflict between parents will leave scars. Try to practice damage control!

2. Young children need regular schedules and routines to make them feel safe. Changing routines can cause confusion and distress. Although divorce is an unstable period in your life, try to provide a stable home for your child with routine, consistency, and appropriate discipline. Ideally, both parents keep the same routine with young children. Writing routines in a notebook, which goes back and forth with the child, is a way of communicating daily routines. Practically, you can't control what happens in the house of the other parent, but at least try to keep consistency in your home (and hope the other parent will do the same).

3. Don't feel guilty for setting boundaries to your child's behavior because he or she is "going through so much already." Children need limits and structure as much as positive reinforcement. This increases their sense of safety and self-esteem.

4. Don't ask your child to choose between you and the other parent. Children by nature are loyal to both of their parents. Allow your child to love the other parent without fear of making you sad or angry. Adults should make the decisions when, how long, and where the child is going to see the other parent.

5. Give your child permission to have a good time with the other parent. Tell your child that, although you will miss the child, you will be fine. The child should not have to worry about you; it is hard enough as it is.

6. Most children (of any age) have reunification fantasies about their parents. Be clear and don't feed the child's hope that you will get back together.

7. Young children often think it is their fault (because they were behaving badly) that their parents are separated. Reassure your child that it is not his or her fault. Explain that separation is your choice, you and the other parent didn't get along, and both parents think this is better for all of you. Young children don't need to know details about the reason for divorce. Even if parents don't live together, they never stop being Mommy and Daddy. They keep caring for and loving the child.

8. Grandparents and extended family are important parts of children's lives. In order to form their unique identity, children need to know where they are coming from. Make sure your child is

able to establish and keep the relationship with the extended family from both sides.

9. If your child regresses to an earlier stage in development (think about wetting his or her pants again or acting like a baby), view this as a sign of anxiety and powerlessness. Don't punish the child. As a coping mechanism to feeling unsafe or insecure, children may regress to an earlier developmental stage where they felt safe and sheltered.

10. Young children don't have a good sense of time yet. Make it visual to the child when he or she will be with each parent. For example, draw hearts for the amount of days the child is with one parent, and let the child paint or stick stickers on one heart every day. Sticking a photo of the corresponding parent on the hearts will make it even more visual. That takes away one uncertainty already and teaches the child to cope. Now the child knows how many days will pass before seeing the other parent again.

11. If the contact between you and the other parent is too difficult, and you want to avoid exposing your child to parental conflict at drop-off and pickup, consider asking another trustworthy person (grandparent, aunt, friend) to facilitate the transition.

12. Even though it is hard at times, don't speak negatively about the other parent or his extended family to the child or to others when the child can hear you. Keep in mind that, even if you think the child can't hear you, he or she may be listening.

13. Don't use the child as a spy between the two households. Asking the child details about the other parent's activities (e.g., dating life) can bring your child into a loyalty conflict.

14. It is normal that your child will at times be upset with the other parent. Children get upset when parents set boundaries. Don't use this moment to fuel his or her anger with your own resentment and frustration.

15. Instead of planning activities or visits, give your child time to unwind and play quietly after a visit with the other parent.

16. To avoid extra stress on the child, don't be rigid in dividing clothes, toys, and other personal belongings between the two houses.

17. Even if you have to fake it, act respectful around the other parent. Remember that you are a role model for your child. Your child learns about relationships, social skills, and problem solving by watching you.

For more information about the author and mediation, visit

www.disputeresolution.me

Made in the USA
Lexington, KY
11 June 2018